Native American Baskets

by Janelle Cherrington

Reading Consultant: Wiley Blevins, M.A.
Phonics/Early Reading Specialist

COMPASS POINT BOOKS

Minneapolis, Minnesota

Compass Point Books
3109 West 50th Street, #115
Minneapolis, MN 55410

Visit Compass Point Books on the Internet at *www.compasspointbooks.com*
or e-mail your request to *custserv@compasspointbooks.com*

Photographs ©: Cover and p. 1: Index Stock Imagery/Jennifer Broadus, p. 6: McCormick
Library of Special Collections, Northwesten University Library, p. 7: Marilyn "Angel" Wynn,
p. 7: Marilyn "Angel" Wynn, p. 8: Susanne Page, p. 9: Susanne Page, p. 9: Susanne Page,
p. 10: Marilyn "Angel" Wynn, p. 11 top right: Stephen Trimble, p. 11 bottom left: Susanne
Page, p. 12: Tony Marinella Photography

Editorial Development: Alice Dickstein, Alice Boynton
Photo Researcher: Wanda Winch
Design/Page Production: Silver Editions, Inc.

Library of Congress Cataloging-in-Publication Data
Cherrington, Janelle.
  Native American baskets / by Janelle Cherrington ; reading adviser,
Wiley Blevins.
       p. cm. — (Compass Point phonics readers)
Summary: An introduction to different kinds of Native American baskets,
describing what they are used for and how they are made in an
easy-to-read text that incorporates phonics instruction.
Includes bibliographical references and index.
  ISBN 0-7565-0514-3 (alk. paper)
  1. Indian baskets—North America—Juvenile literature. [1. Indian
baskets—North America. 2. Reading—Phonetic method.] I. Title.
II. Series.
  E98.B3C46 2004
  746.41'2'08997—dc21   2003006358

Table of Contents

Dear Parent or Caregiver,

Welcome to Compass Point Phonics Readers, books of information for young children. Each book concentrates on specific phonic sounds and words commonly found in beginning reading materials. Featuring eye-catching photographs, every book explores a single science or social studies concept that is sure to grab a child's interest.

So snuggle up with your child, and let's begin. Start by reading aloud the Mother Goose nursery rhyme on the next page. As you read, stress the words in dark type. These are the words that contain the phonic sounds featured in this book. After several readings, pause before the rhyming words, and let your child chime in.

Now let's read *Native American Baskets*. If your child is a beginning reader, have him or her first read it silently. Then ask your child to read it aloud. For children who are not yet reading, read the book aloud as you run your finger under the words. Ask your child to imitate, or "echo," what he or she has just heard.

Discussing the book's content with your child:

Explain to your child that the Hopi of Arizona and the Seminoles of Florida are two groups of basket makers. Today, many groups of Native Americans make baskets mainly for use in ceremonies and as works of art.

At the back of the book is a fun Hop Scotch game. Your child will take pride in demonstrating his or her mastery of the phonic sounds and the high-frequency words.

Enjoy Compass Point Phonics Readers and watch your child read and learn!

4

All Work

All work and no play
Makes Jack a dull **boy;**
All play and no work
Makes Jack a mere **toy.**

Long ago, Native Americans made baskets for many reasons. Baskets were light to carry. They could hold things. They could be used to gather, serve, and store food.

bark basket

corn husk basket

Not all Native Americans made baskets the same way. Basket makers used materials that they found close by. Some baskets were made of bark, grass, or corn husks.

Today, Native Americans still make pretty baskets. They make baskets the same way people did long ago. They still use materials they find close by.

Hopi basket

This Hopi basket maker uses leaves from a yucca plant. She will cut the leaves into long, thin strips. She will keep them moist so she can bend them for her basket.

This Seminole basket maker
coils grass around and around.
She uses a tool with a sharp point
to sew the coils together. She coils
and sews until the basket is done.

Some baskets have birds and
animals on them. Find the eagle.
Do you see an animal with a
shell? What kind of animal is it?

Many Native American baskets are in museums. Some of the baskets are big. Some are as small as coins! People enjoy seeing these works of art.

Word List

Diphthong /oi/
oi, oy

oi
coils
coins
moist
point

oy
enjoy

High-Frequency
carry
done
pretty

Social Studies
Hopi
materials
museums
Native Americans
sew(s)

Hop Scotch

Player 1

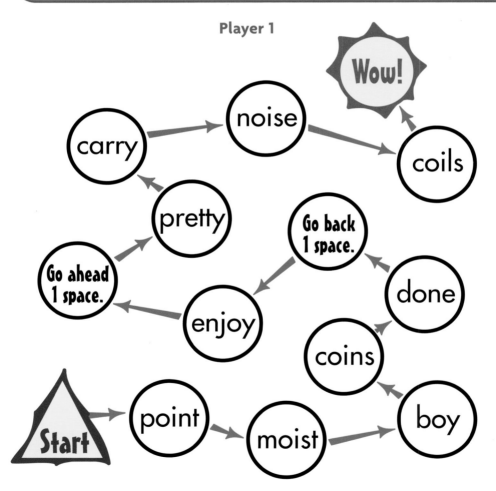

How to Play

- Each player puts a moving piece on his or her Start. Players take turns shaking the penny and dropping it on the table. Heads means move 1 space. Tails means move 2 spaces.
- The player moves and reads the word in the circle. If the child cannot read the word, tell him or her what it is. On the next turn, the child must read the word before moving.
- If a player lands on a circle having special directions, he or she should move accordingly.
- The first player to reach the *Wow!* sign wins the game.

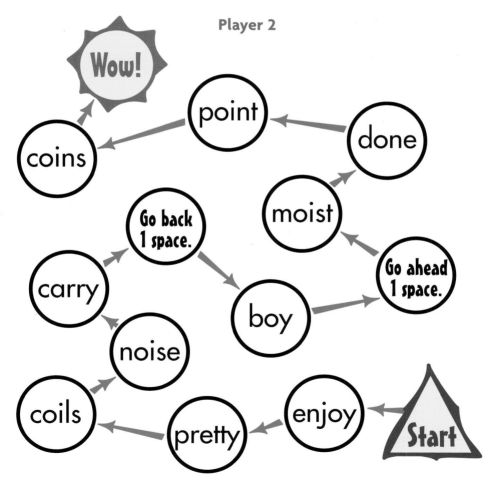

Player 2

15

Read More

Bierhorst, John (reteller). *The People With Five Fingers: A Native Californian Creation Tale.* NewYork: Marshall Cavendish, 2000.

Isaacs, Sally Senzell. *Life in a Hopi Village.* Picture the Past Series. Chicago, Ill.: Heinemann Library, 2001.

Temko, Florence. *Traditional Crafts from Native North America.* Minneapolis, Minn.: Lerner Publications, 1997.

Trottier, Maxine. *Native Crafts: Inspired by North America's First Peoples.* Toronto: Kids Can Press, 2000.

Index